LIFE IN CAITHNESS AND SUTHERLAND

Map of Caithness and Sutherland

LIFE IN CAITHNESS AND SUTHERLAND

Photographs by Glyn Satterley

with an Introduction by Bette McArdle

PAUL HARRIS PUBLISHING

Edinburgh

First published in Great Britain 1983
by Paul Harris Publishing
40 York Place, Edinburgh

ISBN 0 86228 041 9

Printed and bound in Great Britain by
Billing & Sons Ltd, Worcester

ACKNOWLEDGEMENTS

As well as the people who make up the material of this book, I would like to thank everyone who helped during my trips north, especially Donny, Norma and Kirstine McKay of Suisgill for their warmth and generosity; Bette, Donna, Giles, Jonathan, Dominic and Julian McArdle of Wick for their huge contribution, hospitality and enthusiasm; the Hope family and Isobel and Robert Miller of Dunbeath; Megan Boyd of Brora; Sally Tyzeko of Kinlochbervie; Angus and Marina Ross, late of Kinbrace; John and Marie Christine Ridgway of Ardmore; the Roodie family of Bettyhill; Isobel and Alec Ewing of Sandside Bay; Jessie Addison and Lorna and Graham Sawyer of Dornoch; the Clarke family, late of the Fishermen's Mission, Kinlochbervie and Golspie photographer, David Sim.

Elsewhere, I am indebted to John Charity, Andrea Cringean, Malcolm Glover, Monty Parkin, Pat Barr, Michael Wigan, the Cooper family of Perth and, last but by no means least, the Highlands & Islands Development Board whose support made all this possible, in particular Tom Cameron for his endurance and friendship and Allan Scott for his faith and advice.

FOR PATSY

PREFACE

Scotland, which I first visited in 1968, has always held an air of excitement for me – the further north I go, the greater is my anticipation of discoveries. I finally reached the most northerly mainland in 1974, with a complete tour of the Sutherland and Caithness coastline – and it did keep getting better, living up to all my expectations.

My impressions of this brief experience made me want to explore in greater depth some of these areas which I found had been rather neglected visually. With this in mind, I approached the Highlands & Islands Development Board for possible support of a visual study, initially of East Sutherland and Caithness. Early in 1978, they agreed and, following a successful period during which the Board had access to all my colour and black & white material, they suggested I cover the rest of Sutherland. The first project was tackled in three separate trips – September 1978, February and July/ August 1979, the second project periodically through 1980.

With these Board projects, I was given *carte blanche* and was not required to produce any definitive statement upon conclusion. They were happy to have access to a diversity of material which they used in various ways. My prime concern was to make the most of this marvellous resource – a huge platform from which it was possible for me to explore every facet of the scene, the main criteria being visual rather than sociological documentation.

The idea of a book came at the Edinburgh Festival exhibition in 1981 after completion of the Board work. At no time had I set out to create a comprehensive representation of life in the north, rather I wanted to capture the intrinsic characteristics and evoke the unique atmosphere I experienced there.

Though the work I had already done would make up a substantial part of a book, there were many gaps to be filled and, during the autumn of 1981, I tried to fill some of them. Fortunately, I was able to translate many of my new ideas in visual terms; nevertheless, I became aware that many cultural aspects of the way people live in these remote areas are so abstract and intangible that one can only begin to suggest them in visual terms. My hope, therefore, is that this book will serve, not as a comprehensive documentation of Caithness and Sutherland, but as an impression, a flavour of the land as I saw and experienced it.

Glyn Satterley
Sevenoaks, Kent
March 1982

INTRODUCTION

by Bette McArdle

It is just twenty years since I came to stay in Caithness, and in all that time – most of my adult life – I have invariably regarded it as a privilege to live and work in the far north of Scotland. In that time I have lived in the countryside and in Wick, and worked as a landscape painter and a journalist, so my experience of the area has a number of differing facets.

The beginning however was most inauspicious. After a long overnight journey from Glasgow and an early morning crawl up the apparently endless string of villages on the east coast of the Moray Firth, we were at last informed that we had crossed the county march. The news was appalling: a dead land, faded bleak moor and derelict cottages gave way to snow-bleached grass and a slack trail of telephone wires. Under a sky full of fog and scuds of rain the beef cows and North Country Cheviots – characterless animals to one accustomed to Ayrshires and black-face sheep – shivered in the lee of stone walls, there being hardly a growing thing, never mind a tree, in sight. On arrival in Thurso we learned that the bus passed our new home thirteen miles out of town twice a week, but in a few hours there was a bus that would pass a roadend two miles away. It was as we disgorged at the crossroads, in a force five gale with the awesome prospect of an uphill trudge with luggage, a carricot and a straggle of young children, that the first miracle occurred. Someone who knew, presumably from the furniture removers, that we were expected, appeared in a van and we all piled in for a sail up the road.

Things could only get better, of course, and they did. By the time I had learned to cope with that vital necessity, the Rayburn, to catch and release young starlings that fell from their nest down the chimney of the spare room, to stuff up with plasticene the cracks in the window that let in draughts and snow, and to divert a child wanting sweets for a couple of days until the next van called, it was spring and my love affair with the Caithness landscape began.

Over the years, from my kitchen window I saw a field change and again transform. From a rippling sea of ripe barley which intimated the wind's passage to neat rows of daily sprouting turnip, from a soft blanket of lilac shadowed snow to a brilliant green carpet where beasts lay or grazed in a golden liquid light that poured almost horizontally on summer evenings. Though the dead tones and delicate greys of late winter still came round, they were enlivened by fresh ploughing and russet beech hedges, promises of longer light and warmer days.

The furniture, as it were, of the Caithness landscape has more in common with the northern islands of Orkney and Shetland than with Sutherland, which is a high-land county. Unlike the dramatic mountains and moors of Sutherland with its apparently empty great shooting estates, Caithness is mainly flattish. Not dead flat with sharp horizons, but like a gently undulating quilt with subtle, almost organic suggestions of movement. This effect increases in summer when the rising heat on a warm day makes the lines of land appear to breathe like a sleeping breast.

To add focus to this plain there is a domestic splatter of crofthouses and cottages, a network of straight well-built single track roads, variety of colour in the patchwork of fields where the land is arable, and a great range of fencing and hedging. The peat areas are streaked in season with golden whins, white bog cotton, the pinks, burgundies and browns of heather and scrub. But what the incomer and the native alike are most aware of in Caithness is the sky. For whereas the city and town dweller sees little more than the heavens above him, and not even that sometimes through streetlamps and pollution, living on a plateau lends perspective to the clouds and the land, and perhaps one's place upon it. The country dweller is a student of skies – not only the farmer whose work for the day can be dictated by the weather, or the housewife whose washing can become tightly knotted round the line by the wind, but everyone. For the most trivial jobs, such as fetching in peats or coal from an outhouse or milk from the crossroads, require a considerable amount of energy in a three-day gale, and to go to the nearest shop in a blizzard, whether by foot or car, can be to risk life and limb. It is no accident that many dialect expressions refer to the weather: the 'shockad' (peewit) storms of April run into the May 'gobs'.

But visually the sky is seldom anything less than awe-inspiring: the diminishing perspective of distant cumuli lap the north western horizon, mackerel cloud trails huge and high overhead, curtains of aurora borealis electrify the starry winter night, colour and cloud endlessly change through green and violet to honey and rose, and at evening a mist may pour like milk down each hollow to fill the low places, apparently casting cows and farmhouses into the air like images on a china silk tapestry.

It was once explained to me when I lived in Cornwall that the reason so many artists made their home there was because of the 'purly' nature of the peninsular light. Caithness light shares this pearly quality with its gentler counterpart, and from our house one could see the sea both to the east and north.

But if the landscape has its delights, it is the country people that make life a pleasure. Those joint enemies, weather and remoteness, bring out the helping hand, and a snow storm which stops the milkman getting up a side road will bring a neighbour who has been able to get through drifts on his tractor to the door with a crate. The children for years were given a lift the mile and a half to and from school, and there were presents of home-made butter or vegetables, or at New Year a warm newly-killed chicken. Thanks for, say, lending an

axe or jump-starting a reluctant car were dismissed with the expression, 'Oh, it'll let you through'. Getting through what had to be done was the mill that ground us all, and of course it had its obverse side. A doctor of my acquaintance once told me that a good half of his calls in the country were to people who, strictly speaking, had very little wrong with them, but were simply worn down, understimulated and lonely. This is not hard to understand when one considers that a few decades ago the country had a great many more people. Agricultural machinery has brought about improved efficiency in the industry, letting one or two men run a farm where once there were maybe a dozen or more, and their families. Many of my neighbours would recall a childhood between the wars when cottages now used as stores had housed ploughmen and farm labourers, millers and dairymaids, blacksmiths, tailors, wee shops and schools. It was a poor living by modern standards of course, sleeping in box beds on 'caff-secks', chaff-filled mattresses which were refilled each year. One woman told me that as a child she and her siblings had to stand at table, for there were a dozen children and not as many chairs could get round the kitchen table. Tatties and herring, a delicious dish now and again, must have become dreary as a staple diet, though I can't remember a Caithnessian ever admitting it.

But in the 1960s, if a crofter's wife had to depend on her egg money for groceries and pig money for new curtains, I can't recall a table locally that didn't groan. An early morning cup of tea was followed by a breakfast of porridge and an ample fry-up at 11 o'clock, 'halfy-yockens' of cheese, crowdie, home-baked scones and pancakes and jam in the afternoon, and a substantial dinner at night. The social life is still rich, though perhaps not what it was once, when farm servants were hired at local fairs. Now there are still county and local agricultural shows in both counties in the summer, and numerous Highland games and sheepdog trials. Caithness farms mainly produce high quality beef, lamb and some barley for export. In milk the county is self-sufficient. Until recently it was usual to sell animals for fattening in the south, but there is a growing desire to export carcasses on the hook rather than animals on the hoof.

Market days, and especially when there are special sheep sales, are social occasions, as is the dipping and clipping of sheep, haymaking, turnip thinning, tattie picking, or a visit by the mill. In the last decade or so there seems to have been a renewal of facilities in the country, and cash has been raised locally and granted from one or other of the government's pockets to build or renovate village halls. Badminton, rifle-shooting, indoor bowling, WRI and young farmers' club meetings, concerts, playgroups, parties, dances and whist drives all take place in considerable comfort compared to twenty years ago. Then I recall sitting on a hard bench at a Christmas treat in a draughty varnished wood hall watching the children perform on an ominously creaking stage. We seldom stayed longer than the bladders of the youngest would hold out, for the ladies perforce had to use an evil chemical toilet. Later there would be dancing late into the night to a fiddle and accordion band.

Now it's all white harling, avocado and mushroom paintwork, lino tiles and chrome . . . yet the china fittings in the toilets get smashed and vandalism can at times be a problem. This is largely due to the amount of drinking that goes on. Country halls seldom have a bar with the result that everyone comes furnished with their own bottle. The pattern tends to be much the same whether the music is provided by a Scottish band, a country and western trio or a rock group. The men hang together at the back of the hall or outside the door, passing the bottles around, while the girls dance. Often their handbags are piled in the centre and danced round. As the evening wears on, of course, the young men will start to take to the floor.

Hard drinking has been common in the Highlands and islands for centuries: in 1776 there were over eighty stills in Caithness, and it was regarded as a problem then.

Between the wars Wick went 'dry' which simply meant that many people travelled to drink or secretly made their own brews. Stories of illicit stills around the town are legion. As elsewhere, drink is being seen as a problem once again by some, but the extreme tolerance and kindness shown to the drunk, and the general participation in the view that alcohol is a vital part of most social functions is firmly embedded, even although it causes many personal tragedies. The majority of crime in the north is drink-related, such as breach of the peace or drunk driving.

Though I have been talking mainly about rural areas of Caithness, the lifestyle is much the same in the crofting areas of Sutherland around the coast, except that here depopulation is much more apparent.

Despite the fact that the two counties – or districts, as local authority reorganisation has it – make up one parliamentary constituency and have a good deal in common, there are also many contrasts. For whereas Caithness is fairly compact with a population of 27,000, Sutherland has less than half that number of people most of them living around the coast, particularly the east. Where Caithness is an undulating plateau of good farming land and large, mainly unexploited peat bogs, Sutherland is more mountainous, especially in the west. The interior is composed mainly of estates where the yearly round is one of heather-burning, killing of vermin, grouse shooting, deer stalking, and fishing. Here the titled and privileged play and the natives poach, out of a sort of habit. At one time they needed the protein for survival.

But the days of the great estates and their lodges may well be numbered as they become ever more expensive to run, and there is a growing feeling that, at least in some areas, the land could be put to better use, though much capital would need to be invested. In Sutherland particularly, the clearances of 150 years ago have not be forgotten. The battle still rages among historians: some see the clearances as the inevitable result of the changing economic climate after the Napoleonic wars, and while agreeing that it was no doubt disagreeable, not to say cruel, in its particulars, point to the fact that many Highlanders went to the colonies and cruelly displaced the natives there in favour of the self-same sheep that had caused them to be driven from their straths. Others see it as an instance of monumental greed on the part of the landlords, and betrayal by church and state.

Perhaps it was the better quality of landowners in Caithness, the richer soil in the county once known as the granary of the Vikings, or the investment in the herring industry, but Caithness appears to have been relatively free of this bitter experience.

It wasn't just the people that were cleared out by sheep: they are also probably one of the reasons for the far north being quite so short on trees. At one time both counties were covered in woodland and deeper areas of peat show remains of rowan, alder and other deciduous trees. A climatic change around two or three thousand years ago started the rot, but there is little doubt that sheep finished it off. Now, apart from areas around the larger country houses the only trees in the county are gnarled and stunted by wind or burned by salt spray. In the last couple of decades, however, there is an increasing amount of afforestation and planting of windbreaks, and this can help to dry out waterlogged areas. The dangers of growing trees in peat moors however is that the roots can make it impossible to harvest the peat in the future. An increasing interest is being taken in the potential of Caithness peat, a good fuel peat, and within the last couple of years one or two peat-winning schemes have been started up on a small commercial scale.

Before this, peat was cut and used only on the domestic level, each crofter and country-dweller having his own peat bank. A few days back-breaking work at the peats, plus periodical turning until the turfs are dry enough to bring out of the moor and be stacked at the door, and one is set up in free fuel for the rest of the year, though many supplement peat with coal in winter. The smell of peat burning is particularly fragrant, and the

sense of smell having an emotional potency beyond reason, it is a scent that must haunt and break the heart of the exile, when come across.

One of the clearest differences between the people of Caithness and Sutherland is the fact that while the latter county was at one time all Gaelic speaking, Caithness has bery different cultural roots. Though not much is known about the Land of the Catti, or Cat men – hence Caithness – it was evidently very populous in pre-history. There are chambered cairns, standing stones and brochs in virtually every corner of the county. A formation of stone rows is unique to the county and the adjacent areas of Sutherland. There are some twenty-five sites of such stone rows, the most recently discovered near Tormsdale having over a hundred stones.

It is thought that Caithness was once an important part of a northern political empire, in the remote past. It was certainly very familiar territory to the Vikings, whom we have to thank for many dialect words and most of the county's place names. These include Scrabster, Lybster, Langwell, Watten, Ackergill, Canisbay, Wick and Thurso. In fact the more I list, the more I am aware of leaving out – one could say that virtually every place name derives from the Norse except John o' Groats, which is probably the only place name that the rest of the world recalls. Even the name Sutherland indicates that it was the area to the south of Caithness.

Many surnames common in the county are Norse in origin too – Swanson, Bremner and Gunn. In Suther-land most place names are of Gaelic derivation, and by far the most common surname is Mackay, so people are frequently known by their first names, or by nicknames. Caithness too is rich in nicknames which express the tolerant dry humour and the affection in which close-knit communities hold their members.

But for the Vikings it was unlikely that Caithness was much more than a crossroads, though remains of a Viking settlement have been discovered at Freswick.

After their influence, which lasted over 350 years, we enter recorded history, and there are many dark and stirring tales of bloodshed and intrigue through the feuding between rival families, and many ruined castles to bear testament to it all.

We moved from the pastoral hinterland into the county town and royal burgh of Wick about seven years ago, and discovered a whole new facet of Caithness life – the herring. Not that there are many of the 'silver darlings' to be seen nowadays. Having once been the greatest herring port in the world for a century is a difficult history to accommodate, and the images of barrel-piled quays, a forest of boats, and fishermen and quick-fingered fishwives from every airt are still quick memories for many. There is a great pride of place in Wickers – in less kind moods one could say that the town has a herring stuck in its gullet, and sometimes nearly chokes on it.

But something of its raucous cosmopolitan air of a century ago may return as – rather late in the day – the town begins to attract some oil-related industry. Since the Second World War the local fishing fleet has seine-netted or trawled white fish and there are still several hundred who depend on the fishing for a livelihood, in Wick and several lesser ports. Elsewhere in the north there is salmon and shell fishing, and many crofters eke out their incomes with a bit of fishing throughout the two counties.

Though its days of glory appear in the meantime to be over, Wick, with its population of 8,000 or so, retains a particular quality in its people of directness and no nonsense. One of the valuable elements of small town living is that judge and accused may rub shoulders in the street, employer and employee may dram at the same bar, officials and councillors can be collared in the newsagents, and everyone gets their groceries from the same two or three stores. There is a workable relationship and regular contact between people face to face that keeps a healthy proportion to human affairs. However, regionalisation and the tendency to centralise organisations 150 miles away in Inverness makes for much buck-passing on the A9.

An instance of how 'improving' facilities up to present day standards can actually mean poorer service occurs in Sutherland in the matter of maternity facilities. Caithness has one maternity unit left at Thurso, but Sutherland mothers face a lengthy journey to Inverness since the county's last maternity unit closed a few years ago. The result is that several babies have been delivered in ambulances parked in laybys. Many Sutherland families, too, virtually lose their children at secondary school age as the only high schools up to sixth year level are on the east coast, and rural children have to live in hostels there during term time. The result of being separated from their families and roots through their teenage years is that many leave the north altogether, thus compounding the depopulation problem.

Though Caithness does not have this particular difficulty with its two high schools and technical college, it shares a problem that has always beset the Highlands. The academically most successful young people have to go south to further their education. This deprives the community of some of its brighter intellectual sparks for much of the year, and often for life.

For most in this part of the world, travel plays a considerable part in their lives – not only for students and those like me who go south to visit family, or for hospital patients going for specialist help, but increasingly for people who want to visit the big stores of Inverness, Edinburgh or Glasgow. Saturday express buses go to Inverness in much less than the five-hour train time, and there are regular coach trips to the south of Scotland. Allied to the increasing popularity of mail order firms and one-day sales, there is an ever-growing pressure on local shops. Small corner shops have already largely given way to supermarkets, but the loss of good shopping facilities in the north would mean a serious deterioration in the quality of life. Good roads can pave the way of exodus as well as improvement. However that is something that has to be risked;

Highland ratepayers pay many times more per head each year on roads and transport than those in other parts of the country, and most people back the plan to bridge the Dornoch Firth, cutting the time of the journey between Inverness and the far north even more.

Probably the most astonishing thing to happen in Caithness since the last war was the arrival in the mid 1950s of the UK Atomic Energy Authority. Thurso had been, for a century, the centre of the flagstone industry. The county lies on a bed of hard grey stone that splits easily, and in the 1820s the potential for export was grasped. Quarries opened up all over, and stately sailing ships left Thurso, Scrabster and Castletown with cargoes of flagstone for ports all around the world. By the turn of the century there was an average of 16,000 tons per year of Caithness flagstone leaving the county to pave the major cities of Europe, North America and India, as well as Edinburgh and London. Many a Caithnessian in foreign parts has looked down to realise that he is standing on a part of his native land.

Though dimpled concrete has long since ousted this beautiful flag, it is still to be seen throughout Caithness in building stone, roof tiles and farm outbuildings that have not suffered the ubiquitous blandness of harling. Outhouse walls may be made of huge flags; it is still common in fencing and drystone dykes; and it is occasionally to be found in town pavements. There is once more some quarrying, but mainly for the luxury market in fireplaces, for repairs in Edinburgh, for paths and road metal.

But the flagstone industry had been dead some decades when the UKAEA arrived with all the pioneering spirit of 'back-room boys' and a vision of cheap power to an area that had, in the absence of coal, not undergone the industrial revolution in the way that most of the rest of Britain had.

Though the site of Dounreay was chosen mainly because of its remoteness from a large centre of population, the effect has been to regenerate the economy of the area. Within a short time the 3000 population of Thurso had tripled, and people travel from all over Caithness and north Sutherland to work at Dounreay. Such a large invasion of a small town is not easily accomplished, but 'the atomics' appeared to settle in well and have added much to the social and cultural life of the area. For their part the Caithnessians have taken this leap into the atomic age very much in their stride. The same flexibility and inventive genius that has shown itself in generations of mechanically-minded handymen – saving every scrap and oddment because 'it'll come in handy supposing it's never needed' – these same qualities seem to stand in good stead for the sophisticated technology of the atom.

Nevertheless there is something unreal about Dounreay. It does not spring from land or sea, and is too dependent on government policy. As the insanity of the world build-up of nuclear weaponry becomes more appreciated, there is a growing unease as the distinction between nuclear power and nuclear weapons becomes eroded. And there is always the old adage about having most of one's eggs in one basket, although Caithness has survived the disappearance of major industries before.

And after all, small is not always, necessarily beautiful. Many small industries have come and gone, that were not sufficiently rooted in the north. Once the initial advantages of setting up, in the way of subsidies, begin to wear off, there's a temptation for companies based elsewhere to pull out, complaining of high transport costs and hard times.

However there are many thriving small firms in Caithness and east Sutherland particularly. Besides haulage, building and engineering contractors, agricultural merchants and ship chandlers, tradesmen, shops, garages and fish sellers, there are distilleries at Brora and Wick, wool and tweed manufacturers at Brora. More recent industries set up in Wick include the manufacture of fine glassware that goes all over the world, an electronics firm that in a few short years has won prizes for its contribution to the oil industry in particular for its underwater TV camera equipment, a recording business that turns out quantities of cassette tapes for a mass market, various small concerns making leather goods and sheepskins, fish processors and boatbuilders. At the harbour an oil-related company has the lease of a quay which can take the biggest of boats. Not far away at Wester the same firm are fabricating pipelines for use in the oilfields of the North Sea.

In Thurso there are meat processing and gas bottling plants, concrete block-making and the manufacture of window units. Nearby in Castletown deep freezes are made for export to as far away as India, sweets are made at Mid Clyth, while in Halkirk there is a plastics factory. The two counties each have their own printing works, producing a twice-weekly newspaper in Wick and a weekly in Golspie.

In Caithness and Sutherland tourism at one time consisted mainly of exiles visiting home, hunters and anglers – the lochs and rivers, particularly in Sutherland, are an angler's paradise. Nowadays tourism is taken more seriously and the visitor who spends some time in the far north finds much to enjoy. Sadly many simply whisk through on their way to the Orkney and Faroe ferries at John o' Groats and Scrabster, or pass by in tinted luxury coaches making very few stops. Perhaps the opening of a heritage museum at Wick, and the proposed development of an interpretive centre at John o' Groats will make the traveller linger longer.

An industry which relies much on tourism is the crafts industry, though the bigger enterprises sell in London stores and abroad as well. These flourish mainly in the rural areas and vary in size from a stoneware pottery employing a number of people at Lochinver, to one or two-person outfits. Besides potters there are weavers, wood-turners, leather-workers, knitters, jewellers, fly-tiers, and exponents of shellcraft. Often the craftsmen or women are incomers, or 'white settlers', as they are dubbed in Sutherland. In fact the two counties have attracted a number of people from the south who renovate old crofthouses and run a few acres.

I recall a scene in the bar of a country hotel one night a few years ago: near the darts board were a group of crofters relaxing after a day's work at Dounreay, discussing how best to fix melamine surfaces in their kitchens and the latest TV programmes. In another corner sat a group comprising a former professional musician, a doctor of botanical sciences, an ex-college lecturer in the arts and a schoolteacher. They were comparing notes on their gestating goats, and how best to polish up a flagstone floor in the porch. It seems the role of Caithness as a crossroads continues.

In fact it is this clearly seen current of human affairs that makes life in the far north so rich and rewarding. Old ways of necessity ebb away, and only an ignorant romantic would grieve for times that meant poverty and oppression for many. Yet as new ways flow in on a new tide, one must be wary that the values of a distinctive lifestyle are not completely lost.

In such a short and rather personal view of life in the far north there are many things I have reluctantly had to leave out. I have not touched on the role of Wick airport in the last war, or the sweeping beaches and astonishing bird life of the cliffs, or the marathon runners that leave or arrive every other day in the season. Or the Macphees, the local gypsy clan who have leapt in fifty years from the nomadic life of tent, caravan and cave, tinsmith and horsedealer, to a kind of social vacuum. I have hardly mentioned language/dialect, or the exceedingly busy social life in the towns with so many outlets for one's interests that there is scarcely enough time to pursue in just one life all the opportunities that present themselves – amateur drama, pigeon fancying, any number of sports clubs from athletics and golf to sea-angling and sailing, arts societies and musical groups of all hues, historical and field clubs, and charitable associations of every shape and size.

Nor have I given space to religion, or a review of the many great men of the two counties who have left their mark, inventors and antiquarians, entrepreneurs and writers, pirates and clerics, engineers and scholars, soldiers and doctors – even the founder of the Boys'

Brigade was a Thurso man. And then there are all the 'characters' and eccentrics, beloved of the province all over the world, though often only once they are gone!

As a constituency with a varied political history I might have brought up politics, especially in view of the fact that the sitting member Robert Maclennan was the first Scottish MP to join the Social Democratic Party. Or I might have speculated about the future of Sutherland where there are thought to be considerable untapped mineral resources, or the rejuvenation of an interest in windmills for domestic power ... and what about the extra-virulent midgie?

My remit here was to give a word-picture of life in Caithness and Sutherland, as I have found it, to complement the fine photographs of Glyn Satterley, which make up the greater part of the book. I have known Glyn for a number of years and have worked on various journalistic and exhibition projects with him. To me he always communicates great enthusiasm for and appreciation of the far north and its people. For my part, I hope that this introduction, along with his photographs, will answer some of the immediate questions, and perhaps stimulate further curiosity in what it is like to live and work in this very beautiful and often neglected part of Scotland.

Wick, April 1982

1. Castletown beach, Caithness.

2   New council houses, Melness, Sutherland.

3.   *Drainage for reafforestation, Moss of Killimster, near Watten, Caithness.*

4. *Evening exodus of dayshift workers, Dounreay.*

5.   *Peat stacker, Achavanich, Caithness.*

6. *Flagstone wall restoration, Shebster. Skilled flag workers like Mr Bruce of Lyth are now a rarity in Caithness.*

7. Wall shelter, Weydale, near Thurso.

8. *Sally and Billy in the Kinlochbervie dairy which has since closed down.*

9.   *'White settlers', Berriedale, Caithness. Mr Whitton was previously a ship's master in the north east of England.*

10. Testing for brucellosis, Dunbeath.

11. *Above Berriedale, looking towards Dunbeath.*

12. Tattie picking, John o'Groats.

13. *Don McKay banking his potatoes, Brora.*

14. Annual August lamb sales, Lairg.

15. *Crofter's sheepdog, Latheronwheel, Caithness.*

16. The catcher at an evening clipping, near Lybster.

17. *Part-time crofters clipping at weekend, Achavanich.*

18. *Latheronwheel crofter and retired postman, 'Robbie the Post'.*

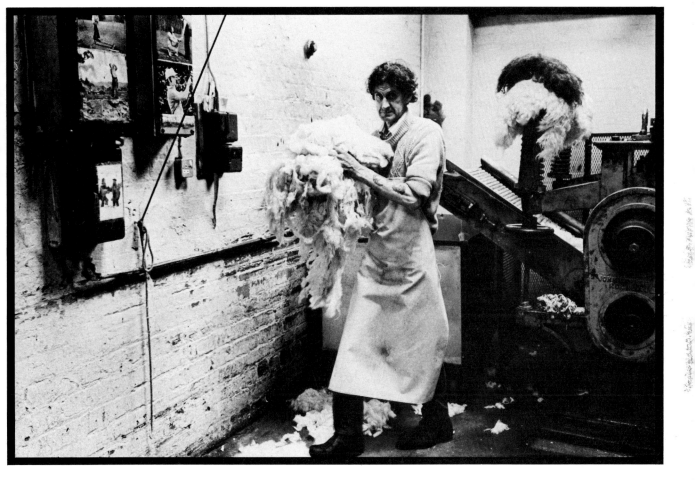

19. Brora wool mill worker.

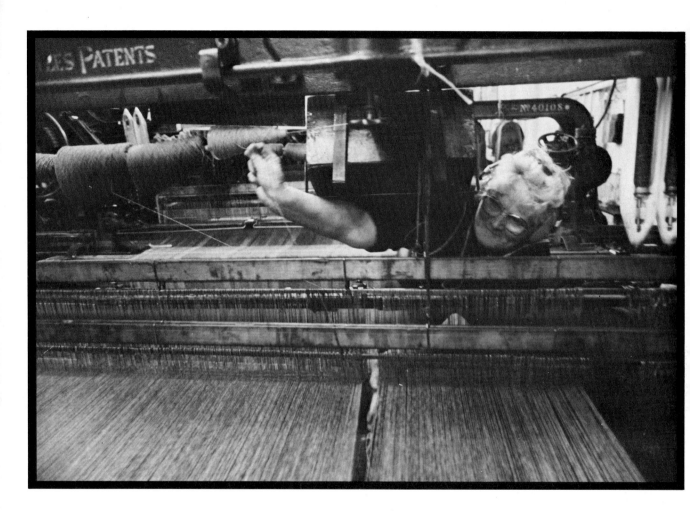

20. Weaver, Brora mill.

21. Jim Bull, Borgue crofter, Caithness.

22. *'Robbie of Sams', Dunbeath, demonstrating his 4-wheel drive, 4-wheel steering buggy which he developed for carrying feedstuffs in winter. Ironically, Robbie, who would fix anything for anybody, has since died due to a tractor accident.*

23. Overlooking the Kyle of Tongue from Melness, Sutherland.

24. Angy McKay, crofter and salmon netter, Dunbeath.

25. Salmon poachers, northern Sutherland.

26. *Waiting for the salmon, Helmsdale.*

27. Donald McKay, once a whaler, salmon netting at Berriedale beach.

28. The Berriedale salmon buggy.

29. Net mender, Wick harbour.

30. *Wick boys netting shoal of herring stranded in harbour.*

31. Landings at Wick.

32. Fish auction, Lochinver.

33. Salmon cages, fish farm, Ardmore, Sutherland.

34. Cyclist on the Olrig House road, near Castletown.

35. *James Sutherland keeps an eye on 23 miles of railway between Helmsdale and Forsinard, Sutherland.*

36. *Tom riding the Dornoch 'scaffie' near Rosehall, Sutherland.*

37. Dustmens' lunchbreak, Rosehall.

38. *Brora bakery.*

39. *On Thursdays, women hand-fold and assemble* The Northern Times *in a Golspie hotel.*

40. Washing day at Ulbster, Caithness.

41. *Megan Boyd, Brora's celebrated tyer of salmon flies.*

42. Tourists visiting Caithness Glass, Wick.

43. Over the Ord into Caithness.

44. Glassblowing, Caithness Glass, Wick.

45. *Pattern cutter, atomic industry
protective clothing factory,
Halkirk.*

46. Approaching Dounreay Atomic Reactor Establishment from Thurso.

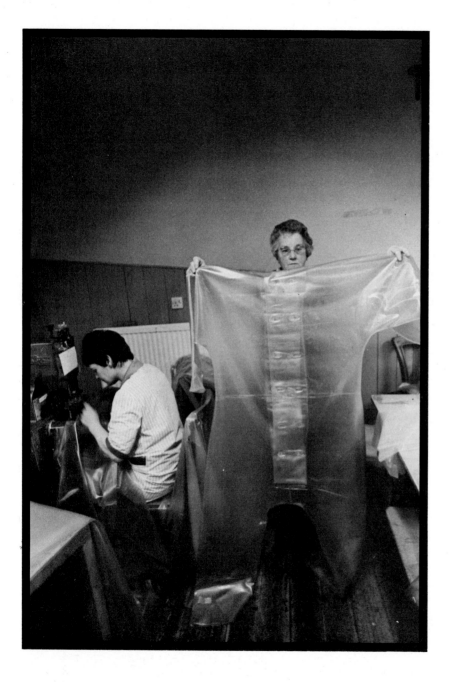

47. *Atomic industry protection,*
    Halkirk.

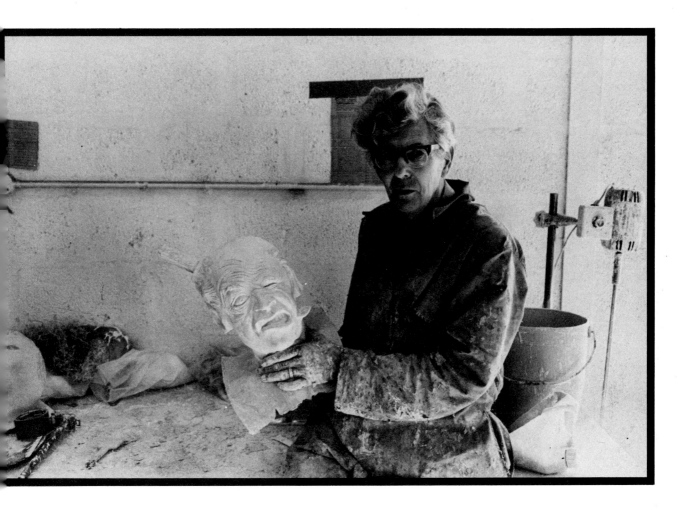

48. Ken Whiley, mask factory owner, Castletown.

49. Keeper with his terriers, near Kinbrace, Sutherland.

50. *Shooting party, Strath of Kildonan, Sutherland.*

51. Stag spotting, Strath of Kildonan.

52. Stalking, Strath of Kildonan.

53. Retrieving, Strath of Kildonan.

54. *The Trophy, Strath of Kildonan.*

55. *'Bringing home the bacon', Ben Armine, Sutherland.*

56. The larder, Ben Armine.

57. Boiling the trophies, Kildonan.

58. *The falcon – a popular new alternative to the shotgun in pursuing the grouse.*

59. *February heather burning, Strath of Kildonan.*

60. Bonfire, Mey, Caithness.

61. November 6, Staxigoe, near Wick.

62. Going to school, Wick.

63. Andy's ferret, Dunbeath.

64. School sports, Dunbeath.

65. Altnabreac school's two pupils and their teacher, Caithness.

66. Lochdu Hotel, Altnabreac.

67. The Camps, Wick.

68. *Inver Arms, Dunbeath.*

69. Hugh Macintosh, The Melvich Bard, reciting in the local hotel.

70. *Gamekeeper Angus Ross's darts trophies, Kinbrace, Sutherland. Angus has since turned to darts full time.*

71. *Ken Butler, who lives in Thurso and is Research Manager at Dounreay, has become the recognised authority on flora in the north of Scotland.*

72. *Dunbeath crofter 82-year-old Bob Campbell's great love in life has been flying; until a friend's recent death, they had started to build their own helicopter.*

73. Spring cleaning, Helmsdale street.

74. *Window cleaning, Wick cinema.*

75. The roundhouse, Wick harbourside.

76. Remembrance Day, Wick.

77. Wedding, Dornoch cathedral.

78. Funeral at Strathy, Sutherland.

79. Church overlooking the old fishing village, Brora.

80. Wick cemetery attendant watching Wick Academy who compete in the Highland League.

81. Roadside graffi, north of Scourie, Sutherland.

82. Charity walker with approximately 850 miles to go approaching Berriedale.

83. *John o'Groats. It has assumed the same stereotyped image as Land's End, either the beginning or end of the 876 mile journey between the two, and functions on the same diet of tourists.*

84. *Summertime lecture at the 4000-year-old burial cairns at Campster, Caithness.*

85. Above the old power station, Wick.

86. *Midnight canoeing, the Trinkie swimming pool, Wick.*

87. John Ridgway School of Adventure, Ardmore, Sutherland.

88. Adventure school classroom, summit of Foinaven, Sutherland.

89. Beach path, Dunnet Sands.

90. *Stone graffiti at entrance to Smoo Cave, Sutherland.*

91. Oldshoremore beach, near Kinlochbervie.

92. In 1868, the Strath of Kildonan actually experienced 'The Great Sutherland Gold Rush' – today, holidaymakers do the panning.

93. Tilting the bucket at Dunbeath Games.

94. Hornpipe contest at Latheron Show, Lybster Mains, Lybster.

95. *Tossing the broom, Dunbeath.*

96. The prizegiving at Durness Games.

97. Prizetable, Lairg's sheepdog trials.

98. Sheepdog trials, Lairg.

99. An objecting entrant at the County Show, Dornoch.

100. *Decorated Clydesdale,*
Dornoch Show.

101. The Castletown butcher in his lunchhour.

102. Horseracing on farm course near Wick.

103. Ten-year-old Ikey McPhee of Wick is already a successful jockey.

104. Stalking pony near Lochinver.

105. Road gang near Loch Hope, Sutherland.

106. Workmens' shelter, the Ord of Caithness.

107. Passing place, Ben Hope road, Sutherland.

108. Warning sign on Caithness border, north coast.

109. *US Navy base, Forss – an American radio station 2½miles from Dounreay on Caithness's north coast.*

110. *Bob Campbell's sports car, Dunbeath.*

111. *Gary Morrison was one of the two 'bikers' of the Rhiconich area. Tragically, he died in a boating accident two weeks after being photographed.*

112. John Bremner, Castletown livestock haulier, with his restored motorcycle.

113. Caravan anchored in preparation, Loch Eriboll, Sutherland.

114. *Whaligoe Steps, Ulbster,*
Caithness. Women struggled up
the 338 steps with herring-
filled baskets on their way to
market.

115. *The Duke's picnic cottage, Loch Brora, Sutherland. A century ago, the Duke of Sutherland claimed title to 1,176,343 acres out of the county's total of 1,297,253 and had numerous lodges built, especially near his favourite spots.*

116. Riverside, Wick.

117. Mrs Sinclair, The Golden Fry, Brora.

118. Portskerra musician, Sutherland.

119. *Leslie Steel, one of two full-time gardeners at Dunrobin Castle, Golspie – the gardens used to employ 35 men.*

120. *Swein MacDonald, 'The Seer of Ardgay' – "I see great prosperity coming to Caithness and Sutherland; people coming back to the area having found nothing but discontentment and emptyness elsewhere."*

121. Practising piper, County Show, Dornoch.